Gases – are they really t

Sometimes
in things th

Invisible things don't exist.
Ghosts are invisible.
Therefore, ghosts don't exist.

Let's look for some good evidence that invisible gases really are there.

1. Take an empty container. Is it really empty?
Fill it with water.
How much water went in?
Did anything come out to make room for the water?
What do you think has happened?

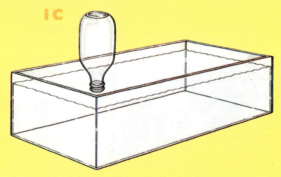

2. Turn an empty bottle upside down and push it down into a tank of water.
What do you see happening?
Does the bottle fill up with water?
Was the empty bottle really empty?

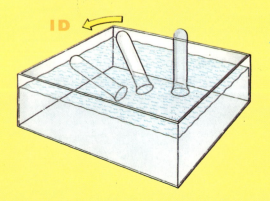

3. Take two test tubes. Fill one with water.
Leave the other one empty.
Hold them in a tank of water, as shown in the diagram.
Move the empty one in the direction shown by the arrow.
What happens as the 'empty' tube is moved in the direction shown by the arrow?

4 Have we found enough evidence yet? What about this experiment? **2A**

When the seltzer tablet is added to the water, what can you see? What happens at the surface of the water?

If there are invisible gases, do they move about?

5 Try this experiment using a hair dryer or fan on the cold air setting. **2B**

2C

There is strong evidence in these pictures that invisible gases are often on the move.

6 Think of other examples that show that gases move.

2D

Are there different kinds of invisible gases?

7 Try this experiment with a lighted candle floating on water. What difference do you notice if the glass cover is placed over it? What changes can you spot in the amounts of gas and water in the cover jar as the candle burns?
What do you think is left in the cover jar at the end? How could you test your ideas?

8 How are gases involved in this experiment?

As light as air?

Some gases are easy to make.

9 Try putting a burning wooden splint into each of these tubes of gas to compare what happens.

⚠️ **Be careful with acids!**

carbon dioxide *from marble (calcium carbonate) and an acid.*

oxygen *from hydrogen peroxide and manganese dioxide.*

hydrogen *from magnesium and an acid.*

hydrogen *from magnesium and an acid.*

⚠️ **Be careful with acids!**

10 You could also use the gases to fill soap bubbles. Dip the short glass tube into liquid detergent and then place the stopper into one of the test tubes. As the gas fills the bubble, shake it loose. Does it rise or sink in the air? Can you decide which gases are lighter and which heavier (more dense) than air?

11 When you have found a heavy (dense) gas, try making a larger amount and pouring the gas into a container with a lighted candle inside. What happens?

12 How could you pour a light gas upwards?

13 Now you could write out and complete a summary chart like this:

chemicals used	name of gas made	with a burning splint	soap bubble – up or down

14 There are other ways to investigate the **mass** of gases. Try this gas balance.

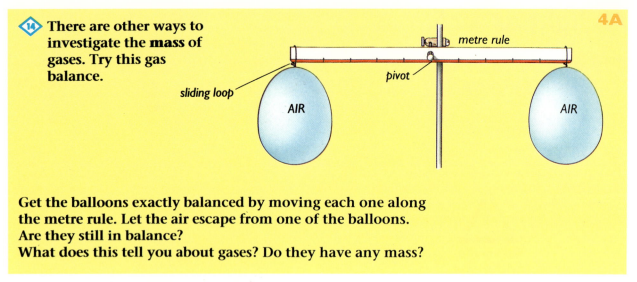

Get the balloons exactly balanced by moving each one along the metre rule. Let the air escape from one of the balloons. Are they still in balance?
What does this tell you about gases? Do they have any mass?

15 Try setting up the balance again, but replace one air balloon with another of the same size filled with natural gas. How does the mass of natural gas compare with the mass of air?

16 What happens when you try to float the two balloons on water? Explain what you see.

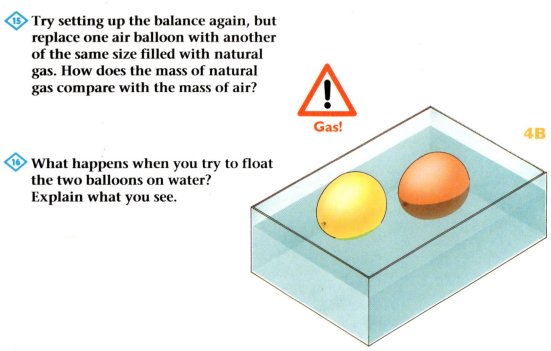

Gas!

17 Can you now put these gases into order of **densities**?

18 If not, what further tests would you need to do?

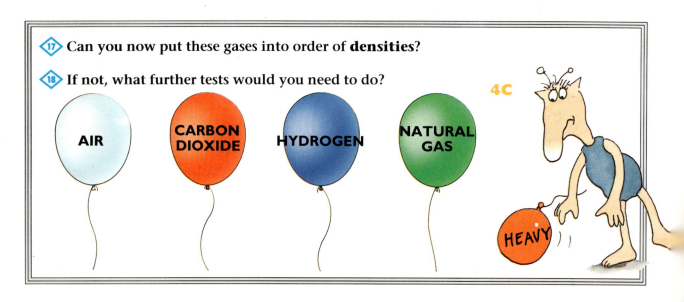

AIR   CARBON DIOXIDE   HYDROGEN   NATURAL GAS   HEAVY

4

Air is not just one gas. Air is a mixture of gases. Air contains two main gases.

More than three-quarters of air is a gas called **nitrogen.**
About one fifth of the air is oxygen.

The rest of the air, about 1%, is made of water vapour, carbon dioxide, **argon** and traces of other gases.

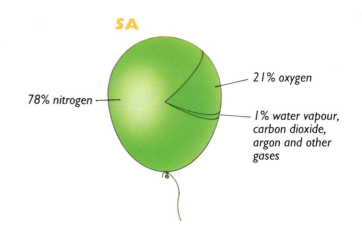

5A

78% nitrogen

21% oxygen

1% water vapour, carbon dioxide, argon and other gases

Testing the air

There are tests you can do for the gases in air and for water. You already know the glowing splint test for oxygen. Here is a test for carbon dioxide.

19 When you add acid to the marble, carbon dioxide gas is produced. If you let the gas bubble through limewater, you should see a change. What happens to the limewater?

⚠️ **Acid !**

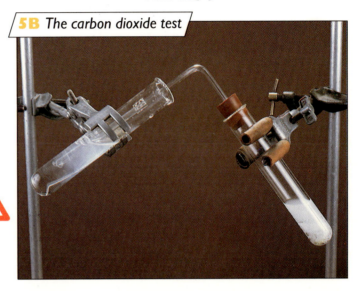

5B The carbon dioxide test

Here is a test for water vapour, which is also found in air.

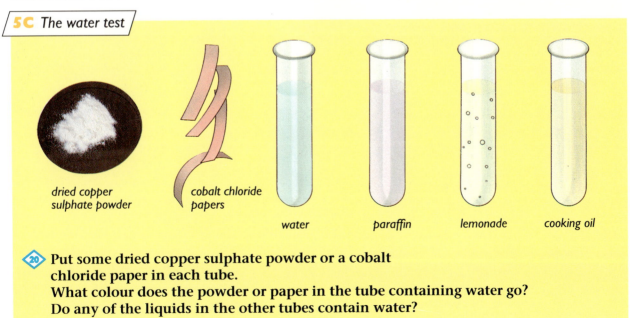

5C The water test

dried copper sulphate powder

cobalt chloride papers

water   paraffin   lemonade   cooking oil

20 Put some dried copper sulphate powder or a cobalt chloride paper in each tube.
What colour does the powder or paper in the tube containing water go?
Do any of the liquids in the other tubes contain water?

Shape and volume

If we have a solid block of metal 10 cm × 20 cm × 5 cm, we know that it has a fixed shape and a fixed volume.

$$\text{volume} = \text{height} \times \text{width} \times \text{depth}$$
$$= 20\text{ cm} \times 10\text{ cm} \times 5\text{ cm}$$
$$= ?\text{cm}^3$$

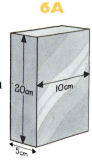

21 What is the volume?

Now suppose we have an unopened orange juice carton that is also 20 cm × 10 cm × 5 cm.

22 Does the orange juice carton have the same volume as the metal block?

23 Does the carton have the same shape as the metal block?

24 If we pour the juice from the carton into the jug, will it still have the same shape and the same volume?

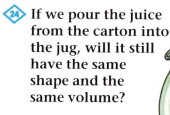

After the orange juice was poured out, the carton was left out in the sun. The last few drops of juice left in the carton went bad, and the carton filled up with a smelly gas.

25 If we pour this gas out, does it have the same shape and the same volume as the orange juice?

Do gases behave like liquids?

Are there any ways to change the volume of a gas? Try these experiments to check.

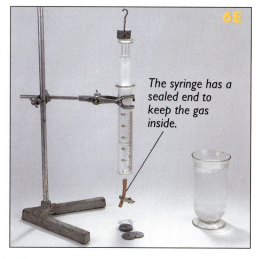

The syringe has a sealed end to keep the gas inside.

ice and water

very hot water

Put the bottom of the syringe in a beaker of iced water. After a few minutes, move it to a beaker of very hot water.

26 Add 10 g masses to the syringe. Does the volume of the gas change?

27 How does the volume of the gas change?

28 Suppose you filled the syringe with a liquid like water. What differences would you expect to see in your results for the two experiments?

If you knock over a glass of water, it spreads out over the table.
What does a gas do when it escapes from its container?
These experiments should give some clues.

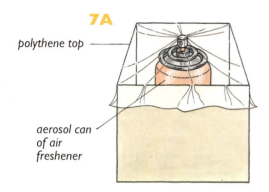

7A

polythene top

aerosol can of air freshener

29 If you press the polythene in the right place, you can fill the cardboard box with air freshener gas.
Can you work out the shape of this gas or its volume?

Be careful when using aerosols!

30 Keeping all the doors and windows closed, lift the polythene top to the box, and let the gas escape into the room.
Who do you think will smell the air freshener first, and who will be the last?

31 How big is the gas now?

32 If someone opens the door, what will happen to the air freshener gas?

7B

The Great Gas Race

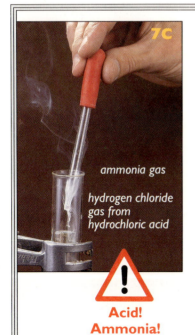

7C

ammonia gas

hydrogen chloride gas from hydrochloric acid

Acid! Ammonia!

We do not know whether all gases spread out at the same speed. To check this, we could try putting two different gases inside a metre-long tube, one gas at each end.

How will you know where the gases meet inside the tube?
Look what happens when these two special gases meet.

7D

cotton wool soaked in hydrochloric acid

cotton wool soaked in ammonia

You need to be patient and watch carefully for the first signs of the gases meeting. How can you tell where the gases are inside the tube? Hint – watch the indicator papers.

20 minutes

33 If both gases move at the same speed, where do you think they will meet?
If the smoke formed in the tube, would you be able to decide on the winner of the Great Gas Race?
The spreading of gases is called **diffusion**.

What are gases like?

We think that gases are made of very tiny particles called **molecules**. Molecules are groups of **atoms**. Molecules of oxygen, hydrogen and nitrogen each contain two atoms. That is why they are written O_2, H_2 and N_2. The molecules move around all the time, bumping into each other and bumping into the sides of any container they may be in.

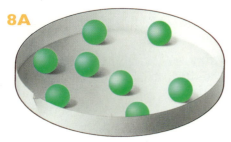

8A

34 Using plastic beads of the same size and colour, make a model to show the way gas molecules might move about.
What happens to the 'molecules' (beads) when you shake them?
What happens when a 'molecule' hits the sides of the dish?

35 Now add some beads of different sizes or colours. Put them in a group together, and then shake them. Do these different 'molecules' mix or stay separate? How does this experiment help to explain diffusion?

The energy of the 'molecules' (beads) comes from you when you shake them. With real gas molecules, one way to give them more energy is to heat them.

36 Can you decide which of these goes with a hot gas, and which goes with a cold gas?

HAS A LOT OF ENERGY   MOVES SLOWLY

HAS A LOW TEMPERATURE

HAS A HIGH TEMPERATURE

HAS LITTLE ENERGY

MOVES QUICKLY

You can find some more evidence for the way that heat energy changes gases like this.

8B

37 Blow up two balloons to the same size. Put one in a bucket of water from the hot-water tap. Put the other one in a bucket of iced water.
What happens to the two balloons after they have been in the buckets for a few minutes?

38 Can you explain what happens in terms of the energy of the molecules of gas inside the balloons?

39 Move the cold balloon across to the hot-water bucket. What happens?

40 What do you think would happen if you made this balloon very cold by putting it in a freezer? Try it and see.

Cold breath

You cannot see the gas molecules that you breathe out. But on a very cold day you *can* see something.

You are a warm-blooded animal. Your temperature stays at about 37°C, which is nearly always warmer than the air around you.

9A

41 What do you think happens to the temperature of the gas from your lungs as you breathe out on a cold day?

What about the molecules as they go out into the cold air? Does their energy change at all?

9B

42 Try this experiment. Take out a mirror that has been kept in the fridge. Watch it for a few minutes as the warm air in the room touches it.

We call this change **condensation**. Where else might you see condensation?

9C

Some of the molecules in the air that were invisible have now become visible.

43 Can you explain what has happened to them? What is it that has condensed?

What's the matter?

The change that you have seen is called a **change of state**.
All materials are found to be in one of the three **states of matter**.

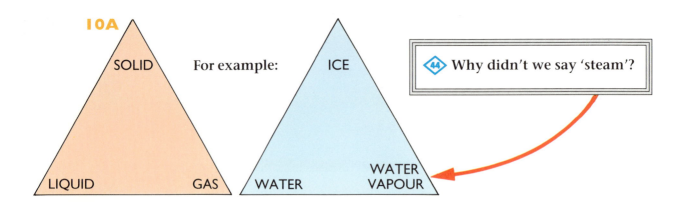

10A

SOLID   For example: ICE

LIQUID   GAS   WATER   WATER VAPOUR

44 ▸ Why didn't we say 'steam'?

45 ▸ **Try this experiment to investigate changes of state.**

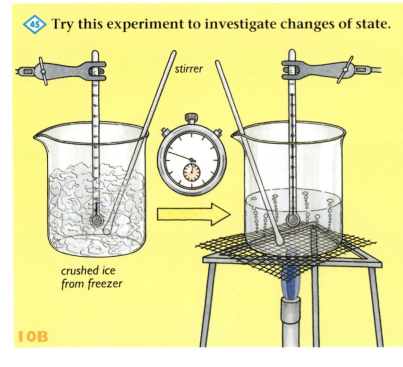

stirrer

crushed ice from freezer

10B

Be sure to keep the thermometer in the middle of the beaker.

Read the temperature every minute.

Keep a record of the temperature changes that you find.

Keep taking readings until the water has been boiling for several minutes.

46 ▸ How does the temperature change during your experiment?

47 ▸ Draw a line graph like this.

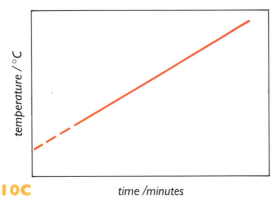

temperature / °C

time /minutes

10C

The container was being heated at a steady rate during your experiment.

48 ▸ Does this mean that the temperature rises steadily all the time? What does your graph suggest?
Did you find any pauses when the temperature was not rising?

49 ▸ If you found any pauses, explain what was happening at those times.

Let's think about what was happening to the molecules during your experiment.

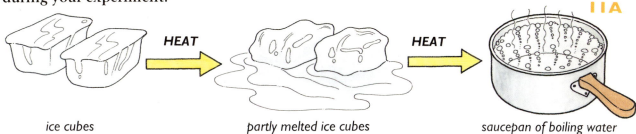

| ice cubes | partly melted ice cubes | saucepan of boiling water |

I IA

In the solid ice, all the molecules are fixed in place.

What happens now to the fixed molecules?

The molecules seem to be escaping.

50 How many changes of state were there in your experiment?

51 *During a change of state, the temperature* ▬▬▬▬▬▬
Finish the sentence.

The temperature at which solids change state (melt) is called the **melting point (mp)**. Different solids have different melting points.

The temperature at which liquids change state (boil) is called the **boiling point (bp)**. Different liquids have different boiling points.

I IB

52 Plot these two sets of experimental results on graph paper. One of them comes from a hot cup of coffee cooling down. The other results come from a hot liquid cooling and changing state to give a solid (freezing). Which is which?

EXPERIMENT A		EXPERIMENT B	
time (minutes)	temperature (°C)	time (minutes)	temperature (°C)
0	90	0	90
1	85	1	85
2	80	2	80
3	75	3	80
4	71	4	80
5	67	5	78
6	64	6	72

I IC

What happens to the volume during a change of state?
This experiment and the one on page 12 should give some clues.

The can is completely filled with water

53 What happens to the volume of the water during the change of state from liquid to solid?

11

54 You could also check the other change of state, from liquid (water) to a gas (steam).

Heat the water. As the water starts to boil, is there any evidence of a change in volume?

Fire and plastic!

In some cases solids can change directly into gases, without melting first.

This is called **sublimation**.

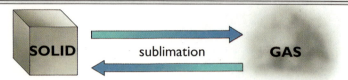

SOLID — sublimation → GAS

A change that can go both ways!

12B

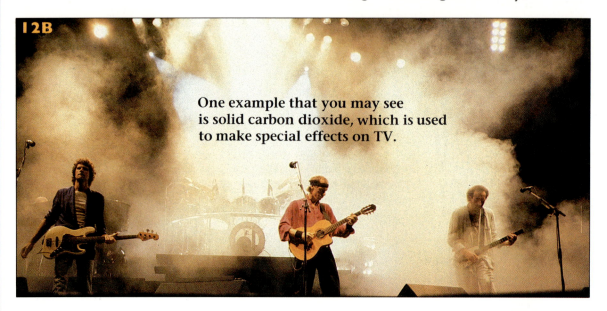

One example that you may see is solid carbon dioxide, which is used to make special effects on TV.

55 Try this experiment. One of the materials simply melts in the ordinary way, but the other material sublimes. Can you decide which does which?

Use safety goggles!

12C

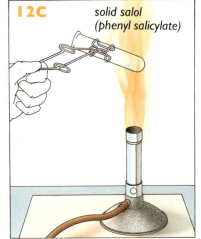

solid salol (phenyl salicylate)

12D

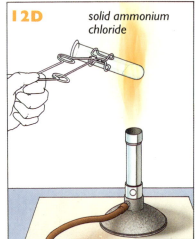

solid ammonium chloride

56 For the material that sublimes, where does the gas go?

All steamed up

Gases can be used in all sorts of ways to power machines and vehicles. One example is the steam engine. Water is boiled to give steam, and the steam is used to drive the engine.

57 Build this model steamboat.

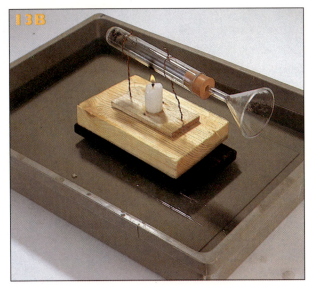

58 Which way does the escaping steam move? Does the boat move in the same direction?

59 Build this model steam turbine. Cut out a turbine from an aluminium foil dish and mount it on a cork, using a pin.

60 Using the results of these two experiments, what do you think is the right order for these different stages?

CHEMICAL ENERGY TO HEAT ENERGY

MOVEMENT ENERGY

CHANGE OF STATE – LIQUID TO GAS

Gas power

How strong a push can gases give?

Here are some experiments where a gas pushes something else.

61 What happens when you try to blow up the balloon? Will the books be lifted up?

14A

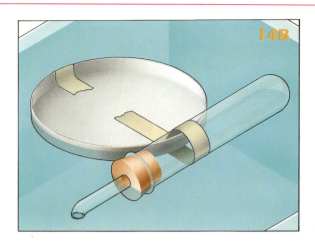

14B

62 For this experiment, you need to attach a tube to a floating disc. The engine in the tube contains a seltzer tablet and water.

63 As the tablet releases gas, what will happen to the disc?
Which firework does this remind you of?

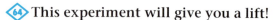

64 This experiment will give you a lift!

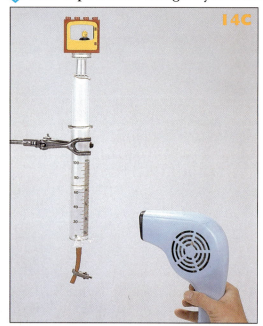

14C

What happens to the lift as the air in the gas syringe gets hotter? Does the amount of gas in the syringe change at all? Is the volume the same? What about the mass of gas inside?

65 How can you get the lift down quickly?

66 Can you explain how this balloon-jet boat and hovercraft work?

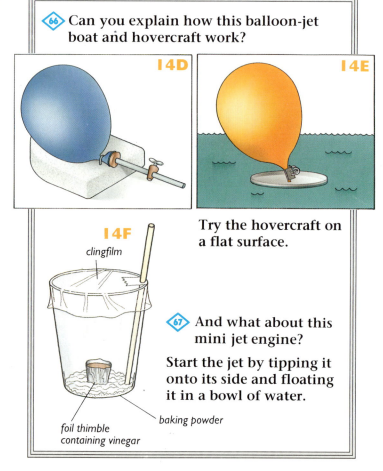

14D

14E

Try the hovercraft on a flat surface.

14F

clingfilm

67 And what about this mini jet engine?

Start the jet by tipping it onto its side and floating it in a bowl of water.

foil thimble containing vinegar

baking powder

Combustion

When certain materials are burned in oxygen, energy is released. This process is called **combustion**. The oxygen used in combustion usually comes from the air.

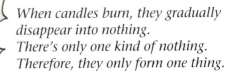

15A

When candles burn, they gradually disappear into nothing.
There's only one kind of nothing.
Therefore, they only form one thing.

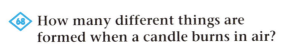

68 How many different things are formed when a candle burns in air?

69 Put the tile in the flame.

70 Have you spotted four things yet?

There may be more than four things, but first you need some reliable tests.
Perhaps you could start by trying the tests for water and carbon dioxide that you learned about on **page 5**.

71 Try them together in this experiment.

What happens to the limewater?

What happens to the copper sulphate?

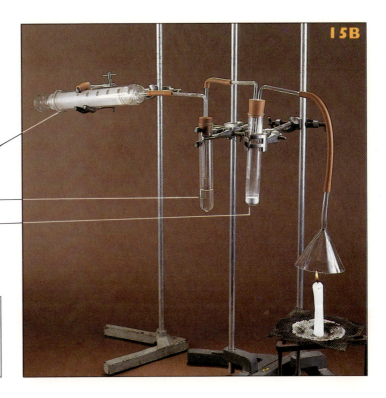

15B

gas syringe (or water pump) to draw the gases through the system

limewater

copper sulphate powder (or you could use cobalt chloride papers)

72 What does this experiment tell you about a burning fuel, like a candle?

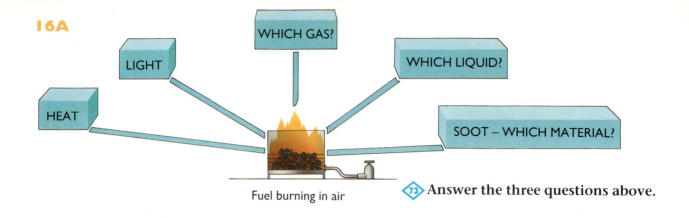

16A

HEAT

LIGHT

WHICH GAS?

WHICH LIQUID?

SOOT – WHICH MATERIAL?

Fuel burning in air

73 Answer the three questions above.

Fuels like natural gas, petrol, diesel or aviation fuel are called **hydrocarbons**. This is because they contain just hydrogen and carbon combined together.

Word equations are one way to show clearly any changes that are taking place.

74 Can you complete this word equation to show what happens during the combustion of a hydrocarbon fuel?

$$\text{NATURAL GAS + AIR} \xrightarrow{\text{burn}} \text{WHICH GAS? + WHICH LIQUID? + (SOMETIMES) WHICH SOLID?}$$

In a Bunsen burner flame there is no trace of a liquid.

75 What has happened to it in the high temperature of the flame?

76 Arrange a Bunsen burner to give a yellow flame, similar to a candle flame. What happens to the flame colour when the airhole slide is opened?
With a yellow flame again, blow air into the flame, using a glass tube or blowpipe. What is the effect on the flame of adding extra air?

Blow only!

16B

Here are some more experiments to investigate the flame further.

16C

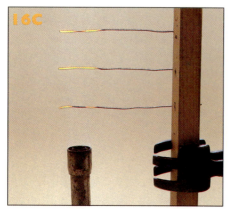

16D

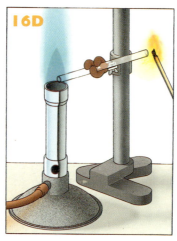

16E

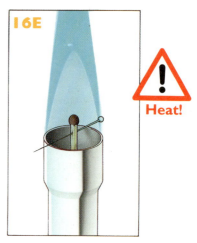

Heat!

77 There are three wires at different levels in the flame. Can you find the hottest and coldest parts of this flame?

78 What makes up the blue cone?

79 Can you explain what happens?

It is the oxygen (O_2) in the air that is used in combustion. Using the right amount of air (oxygen) makes a big difference to how well things burn.

17A

17B

If there is too little oxygen, a dangerous gas can be formed. This is a poisonous gas called **carbon monoxide**.

In these two examples, there is a small amount of air and, therefore, a small amount of oxygen. The oxygen is soon used up in cases like this, and carbon monoxide forms instead of carbon dioxide.
Here are the chemical shorthand ways of writing these two gases formed in combustion.

Carbon monoxide CO (one C and one O)
Carbon dioxide CO_2 (one C and two Os)

Mono means *one*; *di* means *two*.

 Can you think of a reason why carbon monoxide forms, rather than carbon dioxide, when there is little oxygen left in the air? Here is a clue:

$$2C + 2O_2 \longrightarrow 2CO_2$$
$$2C + O_2 \longrightarrow 2CO$$

The fire triangle

Three things are needed for combustion.

To put out the fire, you must remove one of the three. You could cut off the fuel. Or you could cut off the air. Or you could lower the temperature (remove heat).

 How would you put out these fires?

FUEL
HEAT
OXYGEN (AIR)

17C

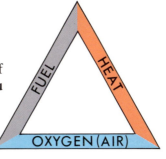

82 Using the fire triangle, explain how each of these puts out fires.

18A

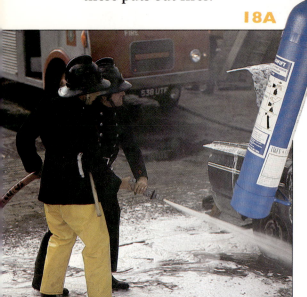

83 Think of ways to put out a forest fire. **18B**

84 There are many different types of fire extinguisher. Try out this model fire extinguisher. When everything is ready, start the extinguisher by carefully adding some acid to the flask. Then quickly fit the stopper.

18C

add a little dilute acid

stopper fitted with flexible tube to point at the fire

metal safety tray

Fire!

weak solution of detergent and washing soda

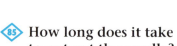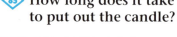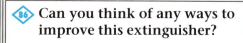

85 How long does it take to put out the candle?

86 Can you think of any ways to improve this extinguisher?

18D

87 Do you remember what happens when oil is poured on to water?

88 How does this explain why foam is used to put out oil fires, instead of water?

Combustion and respiration

All plants and animals need energy to grow and to stay alive. They get their energy from food. The process of turning the food into energy is called **respiration**. Oxygen is usually needed for respiration to happen. Most animals get their oxygen by breathing in air.

When living things release energy from food, they produce gases at the same time. So, are there similarities between combustion and respiration?

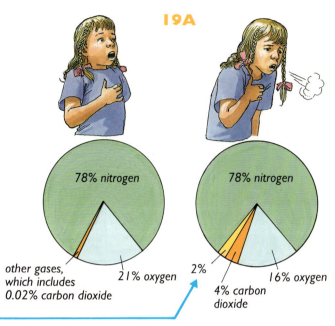

89 Look at the two charts on the right. Describe the differences between the air that you breathe in and the air that you breathe out.

78% nitrogen

78% nitrogen

other gases, which includes 0.02% carbon dioxide

21% oxygen

2%

4% carbon dioxide

16% oxygen

90 What do you think this might be?

91 These experiments show which gases you breathe out. Can you work out which test is for which gas?

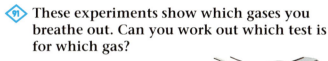

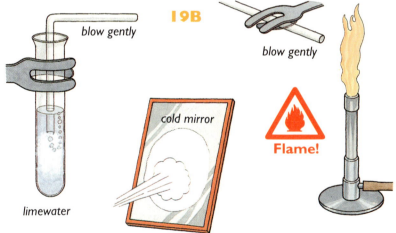

blow gently

blow gently

cold mirror

Flame!

limewater

92 Have we forgotten something else that is connected with energy from food?

19C

19D

93 Do you remember what happens when things burn, the change called **combustion**?
Using these pieces which have become jumbled up, try to build them into a word equation to show what happens during combustion.

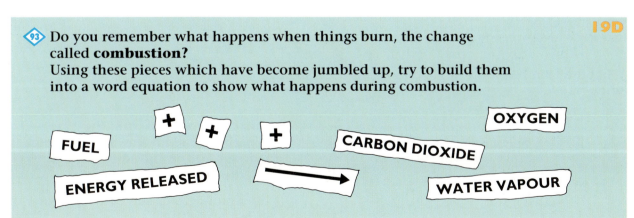

+   +   +

FUEL

OXYGEN

CARBON DIOXIDE

ENERGY RELEASED

WATER VAPOUR

94 Now do the same thing to show what happens during **respiration**.

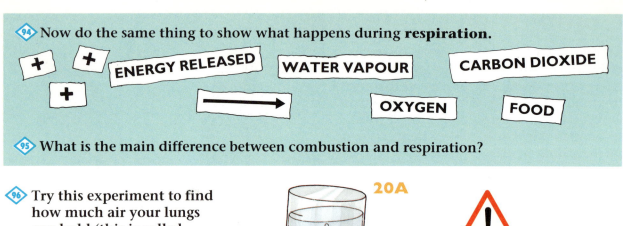

95 What is the main difference between combustion and respiration?

96 Try this experiment to find how much air your lungs can hold (this is called your lung capacity). Just take a deep breath and then....

disinfected mouthpiece

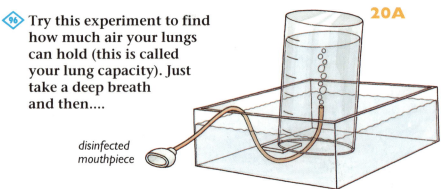

20A

Don't try this if you have breathing problems! Make sure the mouthpiece has been disinfected before you use it.

Does water contain air?

If water doesn't contain air, then it is bad news for fish.

97 How could you prove that there is some air dissolved in water?

98 Completely fill the flask and the upside-down measuring cylinder with cold water. There should not be any gas in either.
Heat the water in the flask and watch very carefully as it warms up.

99 Does any gas collect in the measuring cylinder?

100 How can you be sure that the gas is not just steam?

101 Is there a test for air or for one of the major gases in the air? Try it.

What are your results? Is it good news for the fish?

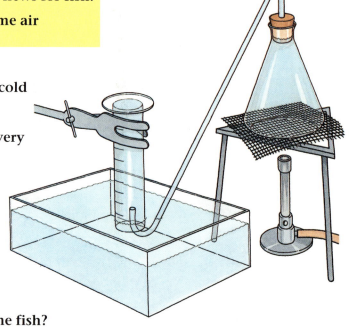

20B

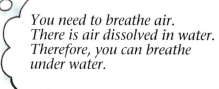

You need to breathe air. There is air dissolved in water. Therefore, you can breathe under water.

102 What did you find from the experiment about the effect of water temperature on the amount of air that can dissolve?

103 Does more gas dissolve in cold water or in hot water?

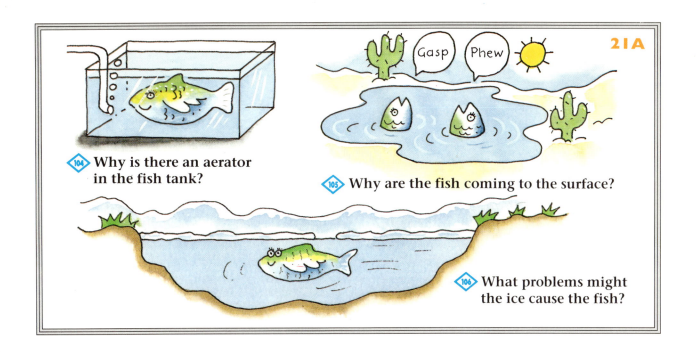

104 Why is there an aerator in the fish tank?

105 Why are the fish coming to the surface?

106 What problems might the ice cause the fish?

What *is* oxidation?

Air contains oxygen gas. Oxygen can combine with other materials to form compounds called **oxides**. For example, oxygen can combine with carbon to form two different oxides — carbon monoxide (CO) and carbon dioxide (CO_2).

107 There are many different sorts of oxides. Try these experiments to make some oxides of metals. In every case the reaction is an **oxidation**.

21B

aluminium powder

iron wool

magnesium ribbon

iron filings

Try putting each of these into a bunsen flame, using tongs or a spoon.

⚠ When using magnesium ribbon, look through blue glass.

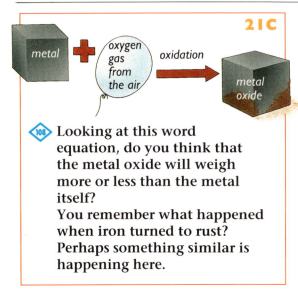

21C

metal + oxygen gas from the air →(oxidation)→ metal oxide

108 Looking at this word equation, do you think that the metal oxide will weigh more or less than the metal itself?
You remember what happened when iron turned to rust? Perhaps something similar is happening here.

109 This experiment should help you make up your mind.

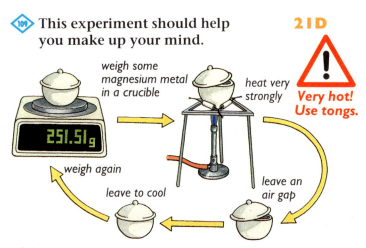

21D

⚠ Very hot! Use tongs.

weigh some magnesium metal in a crucible

251.51 g

heat very strongly

leave an air gap

leave to cool

weigh again

110 Which weighs more, the metal or the oxide that it forms?

Not all oxides are solids. Candles are made of wax.
Wax is a hydrocarbon – it only contains atoms of hydrogen and carbon.
When a candle burns...

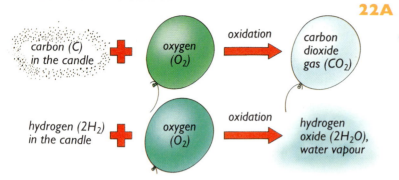

22A

111 Why do you think that a candle seems to weigh less after burning? Could there be something that we have forgotten to weigh?
In a burning candle, oxidation is fast. Some oxidations are slow, like the rusting of iron.

Oxidation of food

22B

As air contains oxygen, food exposed to air can become oxidised. Oxidised food often tastes and smells unpleasant.

112 Crisp packets are often filled with nitrogen gas, and not air. Why is this a good idea?

113 Some meats like bacon are sold in vacuum packs. How does this help to keep the food fresh?

Oxidation and colours

Oxidation is important in changing the colours of many materials. Ordinary bleach works by using the oxidation of the coloured material to give a colourless one.

114 Try these oxidation experiments.

Colour the water in the tubes by adding ink or a dye.

Which ones are oxidised by adding bleach?

22C

bleach solution

blue ink   black ink   food dye   litmus solution   fabric dye

If you wear traditional blue jeans, the colour of the indigo dye was made by oxidation.
Another example of oxidation is the bleaching of wood pulp to give white paper.

115 Find out what you can about dyes and paper making.

The opposite change to oxidation is called **reduction**.

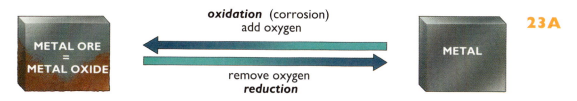

oxidation (corrosion)
add oxygen

23A

remove oxygen
reduction

METAL ORE = METAL OXIDE

METAL

116 Can you decide which of these changes are reductions and which are oxidations?

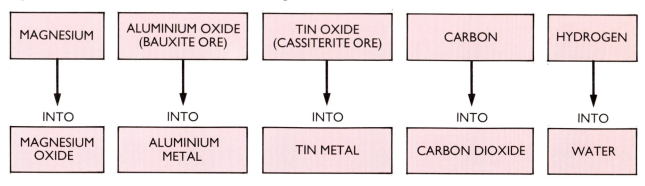

MAGNESIUM	ALUMINIUM OXIDE (BAUXITE ORE)	TIN OXIDE (CASSITERITE ORE)	CARBON	HYDROGEN
INTO	INTO	INTO	INTO	INTO
MAGNESIUM OXIDE	ALUMINIUM METAL	TIN METAL	CARBON DIOXIDE	WATER

Fermentation – letting nature have a go

Normally, oxygen is needed to release the energy in food. But **fermentation** does not need oxygen to release energy from food. Fermentation works like this:

| NATURAL SUGARS, AS IN FRUITS | + | YEAST (TYPES OF FUNGI) | *fermentation* → | ALCOHOL | + | CARBON DIOXIDE | + | ENERGY RELEASED |

Catalysts are materials that can speed up chemical changes but can be recovered and used again. The yeast contains natural catalysts called **enzymes**.

117 What is the best temperature for successful fermentation? It may take some time before the fermentation begins.

118 Which temperature works best?

119 You could measure the speed of the fermentation by counting the number of gas bubbles each minute. Put your results onto a bar chart.

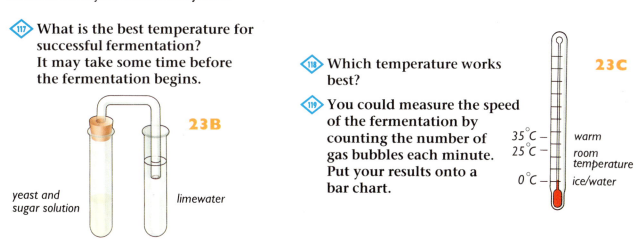

23B

yeast and sugar solution

limewater

23C

35°C — warm
25°C — room temperature
0°C — ice/water

120 When you have found the best temperature for fermentation, set up a larger apparatus and leave it running for two weeks. This allows time for **alcohol (ethanol)** to form. The most that you can expect is 13% alcohol. More than this poisons the enzyme.

Alcohol is poisonous!

There are many different alcohols. The one that was formed by fermentation is called ethanol. In some countries, cars use ethanol, or a mixture of ethanol and petrol, as fuel.

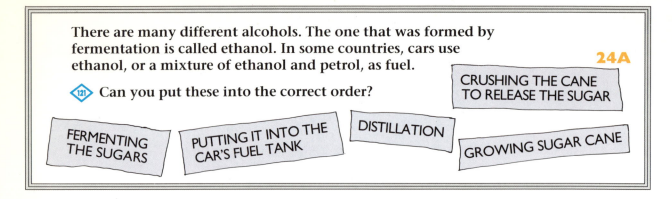

24A

121 Can you put these into the correct order?

CRUSHING THE CANE TO RELEASE THE SUGAR

FERMENTING THE SUGARS

PUTTING IT INTO THE CAR'S FUEL TANK

DISTILLATION

GROWING SUGAR CANE

Ethanol is quite a 'clean' fuel, because it produces less **pollution** than petrol. Sugar crops like sugar cane and sugar beet are renewable – you can always grow some more.

122 Where are sugar cane and sugar beet grown?

123 Can you think of any disadvantages to using ethanol as a fuel?

Petrol comes from **crude oil**, a **fossil fuel**. Once fossil fuels have been used up they are gone forever.

There are other problems with using petrol as a fuel – like pollution.

124 What **pollutants** (chemicals that cause pollution) are formed when petrol is burned?

Petrol is just one of the things obtained from crude oil. The other things include:

- diesel (used as fuel in lorries, buses, taxis and trains)
- gases (used to make bottled gas and chemicals)
- bitumen (used to waterproof buildings and in roadmaking)
- waxes (used to make candles and polish).

Mixtures of different liquids, like those in crude oil, can be separated by a process called **distillation**. This involves heating the mixture and then cooling the vapour given off. The vapour is cooled until it turns into a liquid. This liquid, called the **distillate**, is then collected.

24B

condenser

distillate

The picture shows an example of laboratory distillation equipment.

125 What do you think the condenser does?